THE TASTE OF LOVE

Demba Sylla

we would put our lives on the line
for those we love
yet they are the ones
that kill us in the end

- the taste of love

Content

The Book of Love

The Book of Pain

The Book of Hope

THE BOOK OF LOVE

enter in this city of love
eat from it everything that
your heart desperately craves
so long as before passing the gates
you leave any last drop
of pride outside
any hatred carried
destroy it all
remove everything at the gates
even the bandage on your wounds
and the stitches keeping your
shattered soul in one piece
you can only come in
once completely naked
because you will not be built
until you are in ruins

every morning eat honey
close your eyes
witness its wonderful taste on the tongue
reflect upon it
make a vow to never forget such sweetness
when you speak to others
this is the taste of love

i vow to fall in love
countless times every day
with shadows
with skylines
with coffee
with books
but i also vow
to never hold onto anything too tightly
letting things go when need be

the vow

here's some happiness
don't run away from it
here's some pain
don't turn your back to it
they are like twin sisters
one never comes without the other
they're the sun and the water
you need both to grow
to flourish and reach
beauty in spirit and soul
don't let them drip on top of your heart
like water on stone
turn around and face it all
open the door
let them enter and fill this heart
if not
how would a cup
which remains upside down
ever be filled

the opening

Say you love me
Say it in Greek, in French
Say it to me in Arabic
It doesn't matter which language you use
Our hearts speak a universal tongue
It doesn't matter where you come from
We both live on this planet called earth
It doesn't matter the colour of your skin
We are both known as human beings

she asked
what do you do for a living
he said
i am into spirituality
she said
i love you
but my love is bad for you
he replied
love is never bad for anyone
the real evil is
in the way we use love

love is a capricious thing indeed
you should not hold it too tight
or else it will want to get loose
and you should not hold it too light
or else it may slip away and be forever lost

You have drowned me
I have been immersed
In your ocean of love
To the point where
I do not see
I do not hear
I do not feel
I do not touch
a thing
Without being
Reminded of you.

I must admit
My love has become comparable
To the need felt
By a drowning person
Who desperately needs assistance
This need erases all desires
Except the one for you

even covered in dust
your beauty still shines
eyes full of lust
i'm all yours
if you'll only be mine

all of a sudden
like being relieved of a burden
everything that i ever wanted
finally came to be true
at a time when least expected
i found it all in you

Consider how you love
It shouldn't be centered on yourself
This would push you into
Solely liking what resembles you
And would make you only marry the ideas
That are similar to yours
To only like what resembles you
Is to only like yourself
Do not call this love

friendship is a perfect form of love
it is the unconditional sharing
of common interests
the ability to tell someone
I love you
even if the world was to turn against you
and swear to them
I'll always be there for you
even when no one else does
and actually putting on ourselves
to take them on our shoulders
in their times of need
without them having to remind us
of the promise once made

always and forever

i would hold your hand
And follow you to
The edge of the world
And jump with you

i love getting lost
when looking into your eyes
hoping that I can see my reflection in them
I love listening to the words
coming out of your mouth
they are the lyrics
and your laugh is the sweet melody
of a catchy song
that i can't stop playing in my head

do not cause grief
to anyone's heart
they may love you
as a dying person loves life
they may admire and look at you
as a child looks up to his father
they may be desperate
for one of your smiles
or just a glance at them
in the same manner a secret lover
longs for a sign from their beloved
yet in all this
their shyness may prevent them
from opening the door behind which
their love for you remains
so tenderly preserved

love is the bridge across the river
it is the union of two lands
foreign to one another
cross it and come my way
i vow to meet you halfway
so we can finally learn to hold hands

it is the echo in the air
when my soul screams
in search of true love
i haven't found it yet
but i always get reminded it is there

somewhere

Cast your spell
Imprison my heart
And keep me in your jail
I never want to be set free
As long as it costs me your love

i was at peace
until you conquered my sight
without waging any war
the day you set your ardent eyes
on my frozen land
it all melted away
and anywhere near its waters
the sole reflection
that can now be seen
is the shape of your face

to have it all
without necessarily
owning much

love

she tasted like love
as the ground drank her tears
not because
she had finally fallen in love
but because
love finally fell for her too

the tears of love

when flowers make love to the sun
they never get tired of it
but as in any relationship
they know that it is unhealthy
to be seeing each other with no rest
hence why nighttime is required
and it is to the befriended moon and stars
that these flowers recount
all their beautiful tales of love
thus, quietly brightening the darkness of the night

o my beloved
i am the journey
and you are the destination
every path leads only to you

on the path of love

grab me sweet one
put your arms around my mind
on my heart
slowly tie a knot
and on my lips
leave a soft kiss
that i shall never miss

neither time
nor want for another
would be able
to take me away from my lover

the most precious treasures are hidden
ever so rare
in an ocean of things
they are veiled
covered and difficult
for foolish eyes to see
therefore
look for the pearl
not the sea

live in this moment
embrace it
reflect upon it
and realize that
it ought not be wasted
for
never ever
will this precise moment
be lived again
by you
nor by anyone else
in the same way
that
you are living it now

the present

do not believe
What they say
yes
love can be bought
its price is your heart

A heart for a heart

i could feel
the tears in her words
coming from
the depths of her soul
as we drowned
in an ocean of love

titanic-like

You can love wealth
But never get too attached
Remember that things do not love back
People do
Once you learn to love the right ones

differentiating

What they tell me now
Is that loving you isn't good enough
That you don't deserve me
That I could do better
That I am too good for you
And that I should do better

But where were they
When I was wandering on my own
Through the lonely streets of life
All this time
Like an abandoned dog
With nothing but love
And affection to give

I was lost and had no purpose
No one cared to look for me then
Nobody was willing to open their door
And let me in
Until you found me
And gave shelter to this broken heart
Now being with you
Can only feel like home

All I can see and say
Is that you are the one
And to everyone else
I remain deaf and blind

drunk on love

those who only carry good thoughts
then no curse
and no evil
will reach them in their being
this is why we should always
bless our friends and also our enemies

desirable egoism

I am going to be what I was always meant to be
I am going to love myself the way I was made

I am going to caress and admire my skin
I will fall in love with it all over again every morning

Because it is my own, my very own
No one else can claim it,
And what is unique is rare
No matter how anyone else feels about it

Thanks for being mine,
Thanks for never leaving me,
Like others have done in the past

I know that no matter what,
We will always be one,
Until death do us part.

When life teaches us, its first lesson is love.
A year, twelve months, four seasons,
And I have chosen July for a reason

A time when bodies are uncovered,
And the hearts meet for fun,
When the rays of the sun
Brighten the pale blue sky,
And when running children laughing
Illuminate the faces of the wind.

When the night refreshes from the heat of noon,
When the moon enlightens the darkness of the night,
Telling the stars to come together
And watch over those asleep.

Dawn will mark the end of a cycle
of glittering magnificence,
And will point the beginning of a new adventure,
one of equal resplendence,
A beautiful rebirth, in other words a second chance,
To make the very next day,
a better hour than the one in advance.

I attend the show,
and meditate on this situation: so repetitive,
And yet every day, it seems to me, so unique.

But let us never take a day for granted,
And beware of the darkness of the night,
For in any case, tomorrow is never promised.

my favorite part of myself
is giving it away
freely to you

the sun rises and sets
each day without asking me
for a thing in return

i have learned much
from that single
selfless
gesture
alone

you are the smiles on my face
you are the happy tears in my eyes
you are the heartbeats in my chest
you are the faith in my soul
you are the air to each breath i take
and when we're far from each other
i close my eyes so i can see clear
the thought of you is my source of light
when everything else turns dark
nothing tastes like your love
and you taste like nothing that i have ever known before
you are my world and so much more

the taste of love

THE BOOK OF PAIN

he said *tell me*
what has been your biggest controversy?
love i replied

your love
was a mixture
of poison and honey
you made me drink it all
and I enjoyed the sweet taste
it became the death of me

the pain of love

too often
do we fall in love
with roads
that lead to nowhere

we always want what doesn't want us
our eyes grow heavy
and our hearts grow tired
waiting for something
that was never there to begin with

i sometimes feel like
my veins have lost their purpose
my blood couldn't possibly flow the same
when your hands are so far away from mine
and of all these lines in my hands
can't a single one trace me back to you?

as with money
we are quick in asking for love
yet slow
when it comes to giving it back

it is with affection that I write to you, sweet dove
you being far from me is painful,
and a sour way to love
yet it is not my first time,
going through such difficult experience
when the fire of love increases,
and burns because of the absence

memories of our beautiful moments
tend to become more persistent
as I see you in everything
especially the places we used to sit around
for that which is lost, or hard to reach
is what the soul is inclined to really want

the beautiful thoughts and dreams of you
shall stay with me as I carry them to my grave
for if there is one thing certain
it is that i know how to love best
when away from that which I desperately crave

the absence

maybe we were never destined to be together
only from afar, love each other
time and distance can mend a broken heart
but never fully heal the damaged part
sometimes it needs to remain
permanently scarred

having a passion helps
it helps in avoiding more problems
it leaves less time for troubled thoughts
those painful recalls and sad memories
of the broken pieces to a love story
but the thoughts never truly go away
they just fall asleep and can be awakened
at the slightest noise coming from them

the day you found someone else
my heart blead dry
and i used its blood
to permanently ink the pain of my loss
until the pen got tired
and begged my hand to stop
i then knew that time was up
life still went on
and i had to move on

have you ever loved
for the beauty of love
have you ever tasted it's fruits
it's ripe kisses slipping on the tongue
this sweet taste which softens the mouth
and fills the starving appetite
and when you dare to fall in love
for the beauty of love
on the brain it casts a woozy spell
in the heart it leaves an enchanting smell

but to love for the beauty of love
you may also bite into an unready apple
thus breaking your teeth and swallowing a pain
which at times remains unforgettable

how to remain strong
when all my strength is gone
when it is for you that i long
while to my love you remain numb
i wrote for you a beautiful song
sadly, i will just have to bite my tongue

we are slaves for pain
when we wake up
after a night of love and dream
back to the basics
the arguing
the fighting
the beatings
because that's all we know
it's all we understand
once outside the sheets
an urge to spend our days breaking everything
then pretend to make it all up again in bed
lighting up our nights like shooting stars
perfect lovers
all our wishes coming true
until the next sunrise

- detrimental dysfunction

i know that i am the one who left
but i don't wish for you to find another
i want you to keep loving me fiercely
desperately
unconditionally
i don't want the grass to grow back
under your feet after i'm gone
and it would hurt to know
that you would one day move on
and i know it is selfish
but after me all i want for you
is a flood of pain and tears
i want us to be unhappy
far away from one another
in hope we finally come to accept
that no life in this world
is possible for one of us
in the absence of the other

terribly beautiful things are scary
they always hold a certain darkness
which makes me wonder and worry
I think it resides in their lack of timelessness

so many lonely beings
so many confused spirits
so many broken souls
yet we all carry our burdens
each to different extents
some have even gone as far
as to shut themselves off completely
and for so long
that they've actually lost the key

i am desperate for an answer
to a question you can't even remember
my road of loneliness keeps on getting longer
and my hopes are becoming narrower
i wish i could be deaf when i hear
a laugh similar to yours close to my ear
i am often crying you a river
that indifferently flows in our bed
which turned into an ocean of salted sorrow
i am still desperate for an answer
to this question you still can't remember
i guess this means it is truly all over

i wonder
how many words
have died
in the heart
before they could
reach the mouth
due to fear
or pride

you could see truth in his eyes
you could feel loved in his lies
he counted tales i loved to hear
it all seemed deceitfully real
while losing myself into his handsome face
his beauty casted shadow on everything near
this is how he seduced us all
blinded by love we only regained sight
after he had left us broken and in ruins

after a hurricane

i long for you
after i have lost you
i know
i am the one who left
while you begged me to stay
after me
it was a flood of tears
after me
it was a rain of fears
fears of being alone
of not being strong
of being unable to swim
in a sea of pain and grief
but after the downpour
grass always grows back
you always doubted yourself
and i was always too confident
but today here i am
desperately begging but you refuse
never again you profuse
i guess i sunk my own ship
and while i lay at your feet
there you are speaking about friendship
while standing on your glorious fleet
but your love is something i can't forget
so i will keep on drowing in the deep oceans of regret

every night i go to bed
with my nightmares
every day i drown myself
in the shower
when i look in the mirror
i don't like what i see
i disgust myself
i want to tear these eyes
and replace them with
those of the people
who find me beautiful
 i see so many flaws
i don't get what they see in me
or are they always lying
only to protect me
i don't know who to believe
is it me or is it them
when i am white
i think i'm too pale
when i am black
i think i'm too dark

some days my hair's too straight
some days my hair's too curly
some days my hair's too nappy
some days my hair's just not my hair
i don't like my head
i don't like my eyes
i don't like my nose
i don't like my mouth
truth is in the end
i don't really like myself
would it be in my blood
i am this poisoned fruit
mixture of my parents
but i don't blame them
if i can't fully embrace myself
it's that i have been intoxicated
by the selfish ideals
of those who will never accept me
because a single bad thing
can mark us deeper
than a thousand wonderful beauties

winter has come to my land
you've suddenly disappeared
like a craving once satisfied
the cold is making me numb
i can't feel anymore
but i don't wish for any warmth
in fear of regaining my senses
the hurt would come back
so i remain cold as ice
and because nothing grows
on a frozen soil
all my emotions have died
they tell me it's bad
that i should open up
but why would i want to feel
when it doesn't bring me any joy
look what you've done to me

tell me who he is
I don't recognize him anymore
who's this bloodthirsty beast
feeding off my flesh
and making me live in terror

where did the person by whom
my heart rejoiced
at the mere sight
who was like a swan
as beautiful as he was bright
and who illuminated my way
where has he gone today

his face has darkened
my saviour has become my torturer
the force of habit
has finally betrayed his weakness
or would it be my fault
as he keeps saying in excess

I'm actually dying to believe him
but when I'm in front of the mirror
the bruises on my face
tell me that at this pace
the way he loves
could one day become
the way he murders

For the time being
I have been absent from my own life
It feels like I am losing myself
I think have lost myself

By trying to fit into your world
I have abandoned mine
But now I am getting homesick

You said to me
Don't take too many things
It will slow us down
You'll have everything you need there
So I left some of me behind
And only carried the parts
You wanted me to bring

But love is supposed to be
Two different worlds
Colliding into one another
The good
 the bad
And everything else in between

So how could you truly love me
If you would never take me whole

-I am going back home

When we see each other on the train
Will you really be my friend

When we start talking again
Will my smothered feelings remain hidden

Or shall we just pretend
That this love never really happened
That it was only a dead end

That I never truly cared
That you were not desperate to be held

And that I wasn't slowly dying for you
Or maybe staying alive
only because of you

We both know that
we won't *'find something better'*
Let us for once
stop lying to each other

she was learning to live in a world without him
he was still desperate to die in her arms
it is a terrible tragedy
when love and destiny
can never seem to agree

we were meant to believe in each other
however, with all the lies
and all the cries
you said you couldn't believe in me again
and it felt so wrong
but i was never mad
i could not even believe in myself

the mystery of your eyes
what should i do with it
you don't know
the secrets of your being
dark secrets
and i keep so many

this barrier between us
what should be done with it
standing at the border of your state
i'm crossing the rubicon
setting foot on your lands
look at me

you will have to come forth
if you want to fill the distance between us
you will have to hold on harder
if you want to hang again
to hang on my neck

it is so cold on your lands
what should we do with this winter
can you not see
that from the ground to the sky
everything is nothing but ice
come
let's get warm

you will have to come forth
if you want to fill the distance between us
you will have to hold on harder
if you want to hang again
to hang on my neck

the mystery in your eyes
this ambitious gaze
what does it truly reflect
a strange mystery
which says
that you want nothing to do
with being in my arms again

the distance

He did not wear his white shirt,
The blood was still fresh on the bed.

The vision of the scarlet carpet
reminded him of his misfortune.
So he ran away, in the darkness of the night,
under cover of the mist.

Arriving alone on the edges of the dock,
He presented himself for his trial before the sea,

Which showed him as in a mirror,
His guilty face, lightened in the dark,

Underneath the moonlight
before an assembly of stars,
All silently observant and motionless,
as painted on a canvas.

Against the accused,
The sentence had fallen.
In view of the deliberate verdict,
Guilty, he had been pronounced.
The case ultimately closed.

A Lover he lived,
He ended up sad and deceived,

For every man kills what he loves,
But once the deed is done,
All that remains is sorrow and remorse.

Some do it using a weapon,
Others with a few words,
But in the end, eyes in tears,
They end up drowned,
at the bottom of the ocean.

Her love was painful
Painful of a pain that did not hurt
And often times
What seems harmless
Can bring the most grief and stress
When she stood on her own
Alone in that empty home
The more people came in
The emptier she felt within
For it was missing
The one that could fill it
And make her whole again
All on his own.
She was a pearl
He was the oyster
She was a mermaid
He was the ocean.

maybe our happiness
was meant from the start
but it had to happen
when we each played our part
however we kept drifting
further and further apart
you claimed it was me
i thought it was you
both in denial
yet who else to blame but us
when me and you
is all there ever was

because true happiness
is a gift
that has been wrapped up
with suffering
and decorated
with patience

why the pain

some hearts remain hard and cold
while their souls weep inside
trapped and unable to be set free
acting tough
not wanting to be seen as soft
desperate for love
yet pretending to be way above

and all at once
everything we've ever had
suddenly disappeared
like an entire skyline
swathed
in mist
but
there will always be more
than what meets the eye

the breakup

too often love breaks us
by stabbing our heart
with a homicidal tongue
yet strangely
it is not the impact which kills us
it is the memories

and despite everything
i keep on loving you
because it's easier to remember
rather than trying to forget

my eyes flood with tears
when I realize that our hands
are no longer together
you lifted the anchor
towards new horizons
it is the wind of our quarrels
that carries your ship
while I am drowning
in this ocean of grief
unable to resurface
because of the weight of my pride
pulling me towards the bottom

i'm begging you to stay
do not leave me
stay
even if you hate me
stay
even if i am not the same
stay
even if i had promised to never change
stay
even if your choice is already made
stay
do not run away from me
stay
i know i have made some mistakes
but stay
i still have so much to give
just stay
and she stayed

toxic love

one day she laughs
one day she cries
one day she loves
one day she dies

mirror mirror
mirrors of joyce
mirror mirror
mirrors of boys

one day they're here
one day they're not
one day sincere
one day they plot

mirror mirror
mirrors of joyce
mirror mirror
mirrors of boys

listen for once
just hear her voice
a loud pain in her silence
but it makes no noise

time out to think things through
to think whether you wanted to stay with me
while i was desperately in love with you
or go another route
as if your feelings were like a tv screen
which could be turned on or off
and which let you pick any channel you want
maybe this really was your definition of love
the ability to switch things up
and stay entertained elsewhere
anytime your favourite show would be interrupted
for a short commercial break
and to resume it once it came back on

i long for you
after i have lost you
i know
i am the one who left
while you begged me to stay
after me
it was a flood of tears
after me
it was a rain of fears
fears of being alone
of not being strong
of being unable to swim
in a sea of pain and grief
but after the downpour
grass always grows back
you always doubted yourself
and i was always too confident
but today here i am
desperately begging but you refuse
never again you profuse
i guess i sunk my own ship
and while i lay at your feet
there you are speaking about friendship
while standing on your glorious fleet
but your love is something i can't forget
so i will keep on drowning
in the deep oceans of regret

wherever i have been
it is all that they've first seen
whenever i have a dream
i see beautiful news on the tv screen
but waking up always makes me want to scream
because in all four directions and in between
against me history is still being mean
and i am still being blamed for the color of my skin
as if being black was my original sin

in the dark

every day
i see wars and conflicts everywhere
as long as it's far away
not many really care
the rich are feeding off the poor
in this jungle we call life
because every predator needs a prey
but oh no
this
i shouldn't say
we are no beasts
we are the civilized
as they always claim
i wonder if animals tell each other same

THE BOOK OF HOPE

i hope you inspire yourself
and if you're going
to be influenced by someone else
make sure it's someone
who influences you
to be a better you
not another them

do not stand
at the gates
begging them
to let you in
in reality
the key is you

knowing your worth

you have made it to today
so be delighted
for any day
on this side of the grave
is a glorious one

this is just
a reminder for you
to walk the path
of your dreams

destiny

love of the light
keeps her bright in the night
she dries her lonely tears
for she was sad after the fight
now she looks at her scars
and she knows she was right
to walk away and face her fears
as she'll never let him back in her sight

the taste of love

the birds of hope
sing in my ear
tales of love
that i would not hear
they promised me love
and now they swear it's near
that i should grab a rope
and hang my pain and fear

do not be afraid
of loving and losing
be afraid of losing
because you were too scared
to dare to love

maybe all that light inside of you
burned his eyes
he didn't know how to handle it
so he ran from you

looking in the mirror
can teach us that
both blessing and curse
are the same
and our mind just picks one
to wear as we get ready
to start our day

remaining alone
is better
than not
being loved right

because love shouldn't be wrong

i found peace
in the heart of a street
while gazing upon
a rose that grew from concrete
it reminded me
that no matter how hard
and impossible things can seem
there is a way out
for those willing
to fight for their dreams

close your eyes
when it comes to seeing
the faults of others
avoid the habit
of ruthlessly passing judgement
like those who do not
understand desperate situations
blindness of the eyes is better
than blindness of the heart

heart sight

be your heart's keeper
make it clean and pure
like a place of prayer
the journey must be gradual
so that you may not become arrogant
whoever gives and announces it
is worse than the one
who does not give at all
for to brag is to annul
all the fruits of the gift

giving unconditionally

speak with soft words
use your heart
not your tongue

we walk hand in hand together
through the storms of life
i love you
i will always love you
i'll always ride for you
you've made a coward become brave
i used to be afraid of these things
commitments
until you grabbed my hand
without even asking
and refused to let it go
you refused to let me go
despite the trouble
the strange behaviour
the flaws
the insecurities
the trust issues
i tried to push you away
full of fears and doubts
about you
about myself
about us
yet the more i did
like handcuffs
the tighter you held on
the pressure was real
but for the first time
in a very long time
i finally felt a heartbeat
you brought me back to life

reanimation

maybe it's a good thing
when they leave us in the dark
when we are forced into
creating our own light
it is an opportunity
to shine even brighter
and illuminate the way
for others like us
who had been feeling
hopeless and lost
through the darkness of this world

be inspiring

I looked into her dark eyes
And saw the dream in her ocean
Something so deep
Far away from the universe
Full of stars, and decorated with pearls
I let myself become a hostage
Because nothing was so intoxicating
I am now lost in her world
Nothing is ever the same
No road resembles another
No day is identical
No night is similar
Only the bliss is eternal
Here the moon never shines
Neither does the sun
Yet it's always full light
I can never leave this place for home
It's so full of love, so full of life
I have let myself become a hostage
Flying on the wings, of a beautiful dream

paradise

to lie in bed next to you
and admire such a creation
to forget that time runs away
when you are still
while i stay there
captivatingly guarding your sleep
and if one day
you ever ask me why
why don't i close my eyes
i would tell you that
how could i do such thing
while im with you
when even with wide open eyes
it already feels like i'm dreaming
You make me touch the sky
I am seeing all the moons and stars
that is why i am not sleeping
I swear i still feel like a guest
Every time i hear you softly breathing
in our beautiful love nest
and that is where my soul is truly at rest

blue
is what i see
when the water
flowing in a river
willingly gives herself to the sea

green
like the sight
of nature in spring
after the cold
winter wind

orange
like a beautiful sunset
coming down to its end
as when the leaves
fall off in autumn
marking a cycle's end

Yet through all this
there is no adversity
i can only see beauty
and harmony
in this glorious diversity

nature it seems
keeps on succeeding
where we keep failing
as human beings

differences

Pay attention to the nature of people
Not their appearance
The body is only a cage
For the little bird
That is the soul
If one fills a bag with rocks or pearls
What matters is not the bag
But what is found in it

these are our scars
let's carry them with pride
no hidding
no shame
they are reminders
of everything we have survived
and that pure beauty
is found in the gratitude
of remembering each day
that we are truly blessed to be alive

celebrating life

it was one of those days
until she saw an old man wave at her
with a most beautiful
and heart-warming smile
so she felt compelled to say
i don't know what you want from me
but i'm too busy
i'm in a hurry
and i don't have any change on me
sorry
he replied
nothing
beautiful lady
this one is free
some days
we all need a little bit of mercy

a smile as charity

reflecting on my reflection
i finally came to understand
that most of my problems
along with their solutions
were all coming from
the person i faced every day
when i stood alone
in front of the mirror

the power within

i will miss you
love
i will mourn
your loss
the ground weeps
because of my tears
in the mud
as it buries some of my sorrow
but i hope something beautiful
one day grows from it
in honor of your sweet memory

this sad world
doesn't like seeing your bright smile
because it can dispel the darkness
that is rooted within the human heart
do not let them turn off the light
this light that shines within your eyes
do not let them dry up
the source of life from which it springs

no
never let them dry up your heart
for that is where
your soul draws its beauty and strength

in the power of your smile

i have stopped looking for love
i have started finding myself
i now crave my own company
i passionately make love to me
i will give birth to my own dignity

i love me

while i wait for you
time goes by
and my life with it

for I've learned that
the biggest obstacle in life
is the wait
full of hopes for tomorrow
while neglecting today

the distance from your skin to mine
is further than what it should be
but luckily
we share the same sky
and i know you are somewhere
near the moon
and tonight
that is enough

if you ever find yourself feeling too heavy
i hope you remember to look up and spread your wings
i hope you never forget the strength of your dreams
and that they dry your tears
so you can keep looking up to the moon
while facing all your fears
when you need it
make sure to disappear for a while
and find yourself when others are looking for you
and in the darkness of nighttime
learn to listen to the stars
they have countless stories to tell
despite carrying their own scars
and they are all hidden under the softness of your skin
everything you've ever needed
you have always had it all within

there is a place inside me
with an old box filled
with remnants of broken dreams
they're still there, alive somewhere
under a pile of regrets and tears
but the dust of wisdom is slowly building up.

there is a reason I keep that box
to remind me of the things I've lost
so I can better appreciate those I must
as sometimes, a good thing can be taken from us
because that which we want to dearly love
isn't always what's best for us.

Manufactured by Amazon.ca
Bolton, ON